As One
DELIGHTED

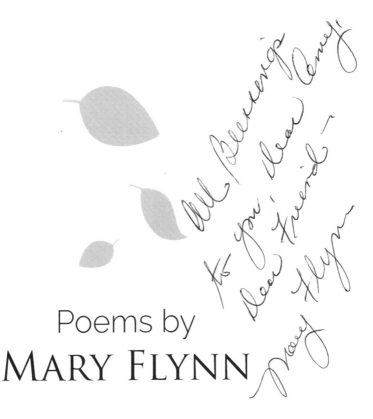

Poems by
MARY FLYNN

Cover art by Michael Butler of Michael by Design, Graphic Design Services, ☏ www.TorqueCreativeLLC.com

ISBN 978-1-7328380-2-4

DEDICATION

To Mommy,
Daddy and Philipp

Other Books By Mary Flynn

— • —

— Fiction —
Margaret Ferry

— Non-fiction —
Disney's "Secret Sauce"
The Little-Know Factor Behind
The Business Word's Most Legendary Leadership

— Children's —
Reggie & Rocky
The Naughty Raccoons

Reggie & Rocky
The Ring-tailed Raccoons

— Middle Grade —
Mrs. Peppel's Pillows

Other Published Works

— • —

The Saturday Evening Post Anthology of
Great American Short Fiction

14th Annual Writer's Digest
Short Short Story Competition Collection

Acknowledgements

I would like to thank Hallmark Cards for giving a young writer the opportunity of a lifetime to work every day with words and ideas along with people to learn from who were much more talented than I in the craft of prose, meter and rhyme. A special thank you to the Sisters at Saint John the Evangelist School in Brooklyn who, in many ways, put good language skills nearly above all else. Thanks especially to my mother and father who gave me my first book of poems when I was a child, *The Family Book of Best Loved Poems,* which set me more than anything on a course for the beautiful shapes and sounds that words can make. And, as always, to my graphic arts designer, Mike Butler at Torque Creative, for adding his very special talent and touch. Finally, to Robert Frost, Clement Clarke Moore, Edward Lear, Robert Browning, Gerard Manley Hopkins, Edwin Markham and Frances Anne Kemble whose certain poems, my earliest, have stayed with me my whole life without losing a single syllable of their beauty, joy and meaning.

CONTENTS

PREFACE

Ever since realizing that poetry mattered to me, I have set about to put down on paper the lines that I believe people would want to read and in which they might find some personal insight, experience, delight or meaning. And, indeed, perhaps something they had never quite thought of before. From the title, you might reasonably guess that the poems in this collection contain joyful pleasantries and images. Allow me to explain why this is not the case throughout the book.

The title *As One Delighted* came to me as I crafted what turned out to be a prize-winning poem inspired by my then eight-year-old grandson. If you've ever watched children at work or play, you know that they delight in giving it their all. In my experience, this tends to be how children approach life.

You might wonder, then, what delight there is in speaking of a dead and barren tree, as in my poem "Spite," or "Spectre," the title of which likely speaks for itself. There's not much of that in this book, but these themes do appear because they are part of life, after all. What's more, as a poet, I come as one delighted to the words I choose to bring the idea to life.

I choose to accept all of the stages, experiences. trials and circumstances of life knowing that God is present in every situation and in every moment, whether it's an unexpected encounter with a hawk, the things a child might bring home, an aging mother speaking of hope to her daughter, the soul of the woods, the cold of the north, lost love and the passing of the years, the beauty of nature in all its forms, and those words we utter in heartfelt prayerfulness.

Having no regard for poems that baffle the reader, I always strive to be completely understood and to let the power of ideas and images speak in language plain and simple. I do not believe that a person who loves poetry loves all poems. I only hope that you will find in this volume at least a few that will touch you in some way. For that, I would be forever grateful.

As One
DELIGHTED

Start of Day

Before the prayer, the robin's song,
the coo of the mourning dove,
itself a prayer on wakening—
delight and sweet assurance.

The hop of the cardinal,
red as the flower you think he is,
tickles the viburnum amid the flit of wings;

Before the imposing sweep of hours
and the blue jay's rowdy squawk,
the day takes tender hold.

« *The Avocet Poetry Journal*

Pinwheel Jasmine

A row of white blossoms
traces the yard,
dense as pillow fluff.
I could purse my lips
in their direction
and believe they might fly,
like snow;
but only for a moment
would I believe,
and only for a moment
might they fly,
for even as some
have feathered the yard
or found their way
to the porch screen,
pasted there like decoupage,

I have seen them
on their fine arched stems,
tough as web-weave,
squall-whipped and burdened
by the weight of hard rain,
undaunted.

« *Quill & Parchment Poetry Journal*

—Featured Poet

At Winter's End

The northern woods
can feel the breath
of new life stirring—
the tiny bits not yet a bud,
the bump of green
not quite a leaf,
branches stretching
like a child awakened
from a long and restful
sleep, white capped riplets
jigging in the streams,
the warmed earth fertile
with humus and loam.

Soon the crocus
and the myrtle,
soon the wild berry
and the woodcock,
the nested bough,
the buzz of the hive.

In the woodland,
sacred and eternal,
cypress, cedar, pine
and fir, ever keepers
of the flame, await.

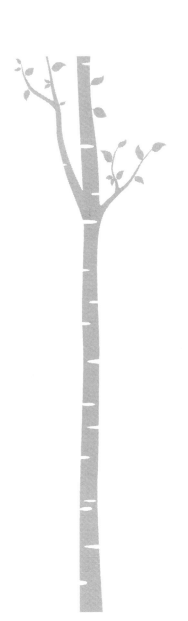

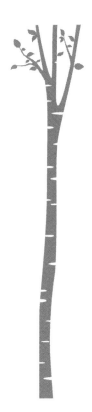

On Becoming Old

I am aware that certain things
will go, are gone – things I did
or dreamed of when my spine
and will were young. I will not
ride like the wind, swim like a fish,
skate for the gold. I no longer wish
to go so high or fall so fast and far.

But I will look at the fire atop
my cake and think of toasting
marshmallows. I will dream and
pray and sometimes, even patiently,
wait with an ever-hopeful spirit.
I will write simple words of delight
and appreciation to my friends, and
maybe not just to friends.

With whatever wisdom I possess,
I know that I have benefited from
frailty and failure, loss and lessons

learned and, most of all, forgiveness;
I see now that it is not about what
we know of the world but what we
believe about ourselves, with mercy
in mind. There is less of me now,
but what is left is so much more
than was here in the half-full
wholeness of my youth.

I no longer care about or expect
the riches of fortune or praise
beyond the treasured accolades
and compassion of those who
overlook my flaws. I will, however,
expect to be surprised. I will
gleefully crack the spine of
speckled-covered notebooks,
and smell the glue before
I patch the teacup.

I will surely forget the names of

things, but words like *more, again,*
and *still* are engraved upon my spirit.
From time to time, I will also forget
what I cannot do and rise with grace
and duty to all that is possible. I will
not hide in the attic or cower in the
basement. I will seek with childlike
anticipation what is new. I will know the
comfort of what is here. And I will look
with delicious appreciation upon what
may come to be the long-forgotten old—
myself included.

———————•———————

Thaw

Driblet, trickle,
rush of waters,
birds in nests returning,
buds and blooms
and fresh mown grass—
fragrant.

Pink and yellow
ribboned baskets,
cool of evening,
fog at dawn,
tabbies dreamy
on the sunbaked porch—
April.

« The Avocet Poetry Journal

Spring Walk

I came by way of the meadow,
past a field with calves at the fence,
a nest, freshly twigged, was peeping,
the phlox were pink and dense,
as if the sky, too full of color,
softly dropped what it could not hold;
the season crooned in the willow,
the morning light was gold.

Before the bright leaf thickened,
before the blossom curled on wooden stem,
before the light grew hard,
I came by way of the meadow;

I passed by way of the garden,
round front with the wooden gate;
kittens, warmed to the whiskers,
slept in an open crate,

as if the sun so full a blessing
could not keep all it had for itself;
a shovel leaned on the clapboard
soda bread cooled on the shelf;

Before the rows grew supper,
before the barrow tumbled out the weeds,
before the dry earth cracked,
I passed by way of the garden.

————◄•►————

Somewhere There is Dancing

That night there was music
in the ballroom on the lake;
the swish of taffeta
the whisper of chiffon,
the scent of blossoms
that surely might have been there.

How long we stood on the terrace
watching the moon move in ripples
on the water, lulled to silence
by the vision of things we could
only dream would be as sweet.

———•———

New Beginning

It's spring! And so with winter's last goodbye,
come angels finger painting in the sky,
and leaves that died as summer did last fall
return to trees that never seemed so tall;
where January's snow had lain before
each daffodil once there is there once more,
as fields awaken from their yearly nap
to blossom in the warmth of April's lap;
and one has but to glance before one sees
birds apartment-hunting in the trees
or children walking fences in the sun...
happy knowing springtime has begun!

« *Hallmark Cards*

Wetland

Amid the reedy redolence,
the swallows whirl,
mellow voices lifting
above the broomsedge,
above the milkweed
and water willow,
above the rise
of their own delight.

« Quill & Parchment Poetry Journal

—Featured Poet

The Coming Spring

On that curve of lane
where the rail fence ends
and the open field lies
beyond the stand of pines—
near there.

Go.

You can see the first
of the purple haze,
the fallow stretch
coming to in lavender,
as though a royal cloak
had been draped
upon the meadow.

In the mid-day warmth,
you will breathe the very color.

———————•———————

For Counsel

I come to the Lord with nothing in mind
and yet I think it; nothing to say,
and yet I say it, knowing that with
and through the Lord everything
came from nothing;

nothing is more than emptiness,
nothing can be genesis—
clay in the Potter's hand, refined,
imperfect, kept and treasured;
perhaps I must pray for nothing,
then, Lord, fill me full.

Seasons

Something old in me
sees Nature's truth
before it becomes
its own earthly spoiler,
that feels at once
the tension and release
of seasons come and gone,
their raging voice
and whispered subtlety,
that hears their thunder
and their song,
that tastes the acrid
autumn burn
and the sweetness
of mown grass.

« *Quill & Parchment Poetry Journal*

—Featured Poet

Spite

It wasn't all that many years ago
that I set it gently in the ground,
tamping down the earth around,
a vision in my head like Kilmer's
—nested robins and leafy arms lifted
in prayer, so that anyone stopping
there could find a welcoming canopy
for shelter, shade and respite.

It stands there now, and who knows
why that every year so far gone by
its branches still so stripped of life,
as unadorned as bitterness,
its trunk gnarled and lichened,
when in April's late-day shadow,
the barren silhouette reaches
crippled and boney across the yard,

a visage haunting, heartless, hard,
lengthening darkly like witches' fingers,
defying springtime and poetry.

« *The Avocet Poetry Journal*

—Tribute to poet Mary Oliver

The Legend of the Bluebell

The world was full of wonder
that first Easter long ago
for the Son of God had risen
but the world was yet to know,
and so to tell of Jesus Christ
the resurrected King,
God made a flower like a bell
and made each bell to ring;
the Heavens' soft reflection
turned each little bell to blue
and they rang throughout the Heavens
until the whole world knew.

« Hallmark Cards

Spring

A friendly breeze,
the warmest this year,
whispered a secret
in the big tree's ear
and the branches rustled
and shook with laughter
and sure enough
it wasn't long after,
flowers bloomed,
and birds began to sing...
the breeze was right
for it was spring!

« *Hallmark Cards*

For Coot

A man of land sets his eye
on fixed horizons; he paces
off his boundaries once
and for all time—it is slow going.

Out where the meadow has
no crest, where the green plain
runs un-valleyed, tall grass
hides the ruts of ancient wagons
that keep him on his course.

He changes only by what is done
to him, and then, cracked open,
wonders at his pain; neck like bark,
fists like stone dug up in pasture,
he brings the land along, becomes
the land in time; it's not the land

itself he says, but what the land
provides; alone like him, it neither
flourishes nor dies off; it is all
rough beauty, nourishing and
nourished by whatever grows up
through it; a good man, like
the good land, the map of Heaven
reflected in his eye, endures
in his perfection.

« The Lakeland Ledger

The Dowry

What will you give him for winning your hand?
A treasure of silver or gold?
Will you give him five sheep or a parcel of land?
Fine linen, as in days of old?
Give him a treasure that cannot be bought
In the little things you do;
Give him the gift of a beautiful thought
When you think he's feeling blue;
Share an awareness in all that you see—
In the wonders of life that surround
From the tiniest leaf to the mightiest tree—
That's where real treasures are found;
Enjoy every sunset, each storm, every breeze;
Take time to look at a star;
And by giving a dowry like this you will find
That your lives will be better by far!

« Treasures-Hallmark Cards

Dearest

I cannot give you
your happiness.
I can only pledge
the brightest of thoughts,
the merriest of hearts,
a passion to seek
what good can come
of this or that and speak
of hope in the darkest hours.

I cannot promise
that you will be joyful,
only that I will try
to be so for myself–
my gift to you,
my happiness.

For Gratitude

On Easter morning in Suwanee,
I look at the glossy river water,
shining in the sunlight, and think of
the fullness and purity of your Word;
I see the things that grow from the Earth,
citrus, oak and cypress, the grasses
and the flowers, seed, root and berry –
and consider my abundance;
I see the birds in flight – the robin
and the pelican, the cardinal and
the mourning dove –and think of
the freedom I enjoy; the ones that
come to the feeder remind me
of the comforts of home; they often
come in twos and threes, and I think
of the people I have been blessed with
on my journey; when I look at your
vast and limitless sky, I'm reminded

of your forgiveness and mercy that know
no bounds; in the morning quiet, broken
only by the song of birds and the flap of wings,
I think about the peacefulness of my life;
on this, another glorious day of days,
I give thanks to you, Oh Lord, for all things.

Garden Delight

You worked there in the garden
where I watched you from afar
yourself so like a flower;
I watched you snip and prune
with smudges on your cheek,
and a few cascading threads of
whitened hair you pushed away
with the back of one gloved hand.

I watched your pleasure bloom
as your basket filled with
vibrant color—hollyhocks,
mums, daisies and nasturtiums
to bring inside and fuss with
at the table, catching the aroma
with a smile and some sense,
perhaps, of beholding a treasure.

I beheld you so, as I watched you,
knowing that just as surely as
the tulips would drop their petals,
so too would you have spent your
time and no more, leaving behind
the sweetness of your life—
my fragrance, my treasure.

« Quill and Parchment

In Time

In time,
things shift,
stampede,
drift,
slide,
revolve,
peak,
evolve,
alter,
change,
rearrange,
move,
transition,
reach
fruition,
gain,
lose,
in time,
but Whose?

As One Delighted

You came in calling, and everyone came
to see what had caused the wonder or the woe,
seashell, peony, splinter in the toe,
wounded finch or alabaster stone;

You came in breathless, and everyone came
to see what you carried in the bucket or the box,
bird's egg, golden leaf, magenta phlox;
their splendor no more brilliant than your own;

You came in squealing, and everyone came,
everyone in a hall too narrow
for us, the snake, and the frightened sparrow,
the neighbor's cat you could not leave alone;
you came in and, always, everyone came.
everyone.

« *The Avocet Poetry Journal*
Writer's Digest rhymed poetry prize-winner

Lenticular Diversion

On Saturday afternoons,
the 23rd Street Theater,
blue velvet starlit ceiling,
red velvet rope threading brass,
gave away rose-edged dishes;
all that glittered was, too, gold;
we went there as collectors
and sat there clutching soup plates
until we came away full,
gorged on celluloid heroes;
innocent expectancy,
since we hadn't yet discerned
the cunning of a sound track,
the artfulness of stunt men
enduring break-away chairs.

Come right home they had told us
but how could we stop the rush—
we were trusty cavaliers,

the mightiest of swordsmen;
with hostile tribes to conquer
wild lions at every turn;
we feigned our great heroics
on the crowded avenue where
we parried and tumbled
outside the local market,
and then behind the bake shop
where a clothesline got the worst.

Late is late in any life,
even Cecil B DeMille's;
my mother set the table,
giving a merciful smile,
and took the plate that made six.

————•———

Muse

I am a slow writer,
slow turning, like the
wheels of remembrance, then
blinding speed, the flash
of a long-ago thing or a
bright idea, a moment, a person,
heartache or delight, merciless
in coming, staying as it pleases,
tickling and teasing, mournful,
soulful, it depends. It's okay,
it's all I have to give and it must be
given, but first a suitable shape,
and how to wrap it and frame it,
fashion both ends, tidy it up, tone
it down, let it out, throw it off,
take it back.

I am a slow writer,
a hard-to-let-it-go writer, forever
thinking it up, working it out,
heart dancing with possibility,
setting it aside until the dead of
night or the high-speed lane or
that intricate task, arms full, hands
wet, greasy, muddy, and here it is,
that turn of phrase, that very one,
happening at will, its own, not mine.
I am a slow writer, waiting, hopeful.

———•———

Sandlot Days

Summer days were sandlot days
when I was a boy of ten;
high pop flies and R.B.I.'s
were all I cared for then.

Our field was an old vacant lot
just right for playing ball,
where my Louisville Slugger and I
went down on many a strike three call

First and second base were seats
from two old kitchen chairs,
third and home—deflated tires
too worn to use for spares;

And, oh, I remember
that nothing could replace
the thrill of sliding into home
or getting to steal a base.

Strange, but after all these years,
every now and then,
I long for the good old sandlot days
that came with being ten.

« *Treasures-Hallmark Cards*

Down in the Field

Down in the field
among tall grass
and fever weeds that grow,
I'd go.

Trees about and those beyond
all seemed to know—
I'd put my schoolroom manners
on the shelf
to play at being no one
but myself.

«Treasures-Hallmark Cards

Summer

The endless stretch
of fiery pumice cools
in the rush of crested waves,
the scalloped shoreline
glistening in the heat
of ever-longer days.

The young birds have flown--
their nests sit empty
in the midst of summer's burn;
the pumpkins and the scarecrows
will have to wait their turn.

Soon enough the joyous
blistering days will pass
to the relief of saddened hearts.

———◄•►———

Where the Pine Tree Stood

Far above the garden
and the rooftops
is a space in the sky
where the great pine
once had brushed
the heavens green;
now the sun, such an
unfamiliar presence
in the bed, as the clearing
is itself, intrudes with
an unrelenting light
upon the vestiges;
a carpet of needles,
a few stray cones, one
small craggy hunk of
bark are all that remain
of the towering sentinel.

A brutal gale tore
limb and life asunder
until the massive sweep,
broken and twisted,
itself became the threat;
amid the deafening wheeze
of blades, great heaving
chunks thundered onto the
garden floor with naught but
the hope of remembrance
for its beauty, shade and
wonder, while the breeze
that once had set the grand
pine plumes to sway
carried off the sawdust.

« *The Avocet Poetry Journal*

Great Light of Heaven

The sky of the passing
storm's dark brilliance
strikes my garden poplar
a rare jade hue; the bricks
along the walkway
luminous pink and intense;
I feel expectant and ill-prepared
for something I cannot imagine
in this moment of captured
glory, in this piece of Time
some say does not exist.

Swift Passing

Something
I first took for rope
for the way it lay there
nearly coiled
upon the pavement,
was not a rope,
was not a rag, though
some part flapped
like stiff cloth
in the wind
from passing cars,
nor piece of box
nor paper bag,
but some small life,
its tail hairs pressed
in the yellow line
like the fern of a
keepsake rose.

The Silver Moon

Sunday mornings we walked the
asphalt lot past the folding tables
and the vinyl tarps strewn with
tire irons and drill bits, muffin tins,
hair dryers and forty-year-old text books.
Pay a dollar, maybe five, and get
the story along with the treasure.

The man in the Gators cap comes
back around for the heavy chain with
a hook on each end he can one day
use to tow somebody's truck from a ditch.
He offers six and pays nine, a price to
brag on later over Harry's luncheon special.

Amid the Carnival glass and ceramic
roosters, blue ducks, cows and pig décor
on platters, tea towels, mugs and aprons,
embroidered vintage handkerchiefs
"too special to let go of" bring the same
price as the large order of boiled peanuts.

Without a boy or girl in sight, grown men
drive a hard bargain for baseball cards
in cellophane packs untouched by
the hand of a child, while the shelves
at the local mall are stacked with
next year's flea market finds.

———•———

Brooklyn at Age Twelve

Come when I call you or
you won't go out again;
look at your hair – when
was the last time you
combed it? Ask Mr. Longo
if the ham is fresh; that's
very nice, but don't get
it on the oil cloth; stay
off Mr. Piro's stoop, don't
make me tell you again;
finish your homework,
or no radio tonight.
If you're good we'll all go
for a walk after supper;
stay on the avenue where
I can see you; you're
going to get it when
your father comes home.

That's the third Spaldeen
this week – money doesn't
grow on trees; Mrs. Kazmarek
said you were making
too much noise in the hall
again; if Johnny Boy jumped
off the roof, would you jump
too? Eat your string beans—
the kids in India are starving;
very nice, maybe one day
you'll be a writer; if you don't
stop, I'm telling your
father—he'll fix you good
and proper. Keep it up.
No homework, no Dodgers.
Listen, if she ever talks to you
like that again, you just tell
her I know where she lives.

The Kid

He wanted to fly, there's no doubt that he did
It would make him the absolute happiest kid;
He would ride through the clouds and brush off
the fluff;
And he knew even that wouldn't be quite enough;
He would hitch onto plane wings and tickle the
geese;
Did he have any parts that required some grease?
He would soar to the mountaintops, buzzing the
goats,
Dip down to the ocean and wave to the boats;
When his fuel was all gone and his engines were
dead,
He would go home for supper and homework and
bed.

———————

Booger Snot

One thing that I like a lot
Is ooey, gooey booger snot.
I like to let the boogers linger
Tip of tongue or end of finger.

I wipe my boogers where I please-
The drapes, the dog, the baby's knees.
My favorite thing, when I am able,
Is to pick a glob at the dinner table.

I wipe my boogers everywhere
Sofa, love seat, mommy's hair,
My little brothers do it, too.
I found a booger in my shoe.

They should have wiped it on the wall.
Sometimes they're just mean, that's all.

————•————

Alphabet Rhymes

Able, album, arid, awl,
Alley, amble, ardor, bawl,
Bellow, belly, bowler, chig,
Cello, chicken, chortle, dig,

Dally, dapple, deacon, el,
Eager, easy, elder, fell,
Fathom, fickle, frozen, grow,
Golden, gotten, gander, glow,

Gated, guilty, gutted, hot,
Heater, hereto, igloo, jot,
Jabber, jobber, junco, kit,
Kicker, kilo, kitten, lit,

Lighten, listen, lively, mow,
Mitten, mutter, mutton, no,
Noggin, nosey, nostril, ouch,
Octave, ogle, opal, pouch,

Poodle, powder, puppy, que,
Quelling, quiet, quilting, roux,
Rasher, ration, rusher, stow,
Sailor, silly, sorry, tow,

Tackle, taller, tasty, urge,
Ulcer, uncle, utter, verge,
Varied, valued, victor, woo,
Wooden, wooly, worry, xu,

Xanthic, xanthan, xebec, xi,
Yacker, yammer, yardarm, ye,
Yarrow, yearling, yearning, zen,
Zenith, zephyr, start again.

———◄•►———

The Missing Board

Halfway down that street
near the place where the El
goes underground
is a small clapboard house
with faded green shutters
and an American flag on a
white dented mailbox.
Windows dulled by age
and soot make it hard to see
the mysterious goings-on.

Around back, a missing
board in the worn wooden
fence serves so well the
fancies of a child to weave
a tale of murder. The old
grizzled man with a shovel
in his grip moves slowly
toward the door of his shed,

the place where he
must hide all the bodies.

Didn't an old woman
live here too? She must be
somewhere in the pile,
along with Mrs. Leone's
missing cat and the school
teacher they said moved
away, but she probably
didn't move away at all.

A much younger man,
no doubt the next victim,
walks up the driveway,
unhooking the gate latch
to enter the yard. He's
wearing a windbreaker,
most likely a disguise that

undercover cops sometimes
use to throw the killer off.

He pats the old man on
the back with a smile, then
hands him a package before
they go in. Just one more
murder the kids will have to
investigate once homework
and supper are done.

———•,———

Smarty Pants

I'll play when I want
And do as I wish
I'll eat from a cup
And drink from a dish
Reach in the fish tank
And tickle the fish;

I'll slide down the railing
And jump off the ledge
I'll hide in the bushes
And cut through the hedge.
I'll climb to the rooftop
And hang off the edge;

Yes, I'll do as I please,
I'll do it. I will
I may knock things over
And give things a spill
Or leap from the top

Of the stairs for a thrill

But even a smarty pants
Plans far ahead—
When Christmas is coming
Forget what I said
I'll do as I'm told
And I'll go right to bed.

The Animals Romp

The Kitty Kat purred her sweet little song,
the hippopotamus sang right along,
the rabbits hippity hopped in tune,
the elephants hummed and hummed, and soon,
the big old lion grabbed his guitar,
the monkeys all came from near and far,
the crocodile's tail thumped with a beat,
the brown bear danced with his big brown feet;
then the parrot called out "What's all this?"
the zebra blew them a big striped kiss,
then the tigers and giraffes sang, too,
they sang and sang till the moon turned blue,
the gopher, horse, beaver and raccoon
all joined in and started to croon;
everything went according to plan
till the skunk turned up and off they all ran!!

———•———

Birdie, Birdie

Look, Birdie, Birdie, look
seed, Birdie, Birdie, seed
come, Birdie, Birdie, come
feed, Birdie, Birdie, feed

here, Birdie, Birdie, here
eat, Birdie, Birdie, eat
peck, Birdie, Birdie, peck
tweet, Birdie, Birdie, tweet

hop, Birdie, Birdie, hop
high, Birdie, Birdie, high
chirp, Birdie, Birdie, chirp
fly, Birdie, Birdie, fly.

Ts and Ks

Words that contain both a "T" and a "K"
Impress me in such a remarkable way;

Truck, for example, is just how it sounds—
Solid and strong, weighing thousands of pounds;

Trinket and Trickle and Tickle and Tick
Feel like their playful, and what about Trick?

It's cunning, deceptive and harder to know;
Traffic is heavy, Tractor is slow;

And what about Tonic? It is my belief
That this is a word sounding just like relief;

Trunk is a captor; it holds what is hid;
You can tell by the thunk and the slunk of its lid;

Ticket and Tackle are hardworking words;
A thicket is great at attracting the birds.

Torque is a technical rotating twist
And may be the least understood on the list

Think's what you do inside of your head,
Thanks is a word that is best when it's said;

There are so many more, such as Track, Take and
Token;
Words using TKs are the oddest words spoken.

————•————

Hurricane Gloria

What light is it
that in a lightless sky
where glow is gone
sets things aglow
before the storm?
The ashen luminescence
of each form
like glimmer
in a maddened eye.

———•———

Fence-Sitter

So there he was, perched on the rail,
statuesque as a lintel ornament
bartered in the West Indies for a Fit Bit
or a pair of Nikes, his tucked wings ribboned
in blurry rows of brownish-grey rick rack,
and as if I were the species in question,
prey perhaps, he put his august head on
backwards, as hawks can do,
rotating it with such fluid detachment
that it seemed about as connected
to the rest of him as a lid is to a cookie jar.
Nature accounts for everything,
although it is still my fence.

He must have sensed my thoughts
the way he took off, banking like an F16,
without so much as a glance in my direction,
his hooked bill gaping toward the heavens
with a screech that shook loose the mulberries,
this diurnal interloper, whose breathtaking

wingspan daily sweeps past my window
in the most ominous of late afternoon shadows.
He would show me.

And so he returned to awe me still,
carrying off a yard snake
who likely lacked any instinct at all
for that visual acuity capable of detecting
a serpentine thread in a chinch patch
from the height of a penthouse balcony.
Who then is the more cold-blooded?
In any case, he is no fence-sitter.

« *The Avocet Poetry Journal*

Debt

We could have put off
just one chore, maybe
paid the light bill later,
paying instead a debt to grace,
in wonder at this sacred place.

There is no bill for sunset
no payment due for starry skies,
the moon its own rare coin
set in the velvet night.

We owe only blissful attention
and a promissory note
to return again.

High Seas

What strength of will that even
in a rage of tides, the savage
northerlies offended to no avail;
helm and hatch asunder
they plied the heaving swells
toward majesty of purpose,
pillager and defender alike
to fire up the cannons;
bailers and ballast
and booty to horde until,
at last, great ghostly galleons,
to rest in tatters from
the wrath that gave them life.

———◆———

The Tug

With a creaky, squeaky sway and rock,
the tired tug chugged in toward dock,
as it trembled fiercely bow to stern,
with its engines rumbled, grumbled churn.
In youth the one-time mighty elf,
now so in need of help itself,
had hastened to each liner's side,
and towed the massive load in stride.

But on this final journey home,
slowed even by the ocean's foam,
the bruised and limping sluggish tug,
could hardly muster up a chug.
Its wounds were signs of what had been,
of playful bouts it could not win,
and now the sea and tug once more,
would have a rugged tug-of-war.

And so, the crew manned helm and hatch
to referee the final match

between the teasing, playful sea
and the tug that hung on stubbornly.
Now, as the sea pursued with force,
to knock the vessel from its course,
with waves in armies at each side,
all that saved the tug was pride.

The poor tug's end was finally near,
and yet, there was no malice here,
for each had been a gallant friend,
a fond opponent till the end.

To this day, that courageous sport,
a crippled ship confined to port,
with battered and abandoned decks,
recalls those great aquatic treks,
and the sea that slowly did defeat
the very life it made complete.

At Dawn - Haiku

Morning surprise
A Grey rolling sky
Quilted thunder

———•·———

Equinox

Come with me,
we won't be long;
the fire will keep,
the soup will hold;
watch how the sunlight
nickels through the trees,
dollops of silver
on the mulchy path;
breathe with me –
old burning, damp pine,
and wood must,
everywhere gold.

Listen how autumn
strums the leaves
in late song
and whistle-whispers;
cricket quiet,
bee-buzz gone;

soon the snow-hush
blown-glass freeze;
soon the weighty
white-quilt warren.

Come with me
while there's still time
for the season and for us.

« *Quill & Parchment Poetry Journal*

—Featured Poet

Child

One day you will take
my arm and guide me
toward the door, you
with your then more
knowing eye and surer
foot. I will see my youth
in you and when I laugh,
embarrassed by my
faltering step, you will
smile your encouragement,
having learned a little
of life and love and loss.

Do not credit me with
your wisdom—grace has
joined us on the path with
blessings beyond deserving;

you will have been my gift and
I yours, for in me you will see
the self who is to come, and in
my peace, learn of hope.

———•———

On The Lake – *Haiku*

Two swans in autumn
Whiten the red-leaf bank
In silken silence

« Quill & Parchment Poetry Journal

—Featured Poet

Wait

"Just wait," my mother
told me, in a very impatient
tone, the fifth time she had
said it; I had wanted the
chocolate cake that was
sitting in the center of the table
—what was taking so long?

"Wait," she said, "just wait,"
on and on it went,
on and on it goes, waiting
for something to start
something to do
something to happen
something to come.

Now, we wait it seems for
something to end, very
little of what happens now
is what we hopefully await.

More important than ever,
it is important to remember
that we did get to eat the cake.
That cannot be underestimated.

Hope – Haiku

On the darkest path
One spark of light
Is as a beacon

For Mercy

You know my ways, Oh Lord –

I am impatient;

I hurry for the ends I seek,

I worry for the goals I may not reach;

You know my mind, Oh Lord –

I am distracted,

I wander through my list of tasks;

I ponder all the things that must get done;

You know my flaws, Oh Lord –

I am a sinner,

I have longings that defy your Word,

I am willful in my needs;

You know my heart, Oh Lord –

I am your Child;

I am weak but faithful – I am yours.

———◆———

Woodland Peace

Give me the curve of a path in the woods
with the crackle of mulch as I go
and the screech of a hawk at the top of the trees
and the scurry of rabbits below.

Give me the flutter of leaves as they fall
let me breathe in the fragrance of loam
give me the solace and soul of the woods
and I'll carry the woods with me home.

Stages

Welcome me now
my life begun,
I, your daughter,
I, your son,
sing in my ear so tenderly,
welcome and delight in me.

Nurture me now
for I must grow
to know the things
I've yet to know
and be the things I've yet to be,
nurture and encourage me.

Release me now
for I must soar,
forever yours
and yours no more,
forever held by being free,

release and wish the best for me.

Relish me now
though I have grown
to who I am
and what I've sown,
a heart still seeking, yet to see,
relish and be kind to me.

Comfort me now
I ask once more,
hold me, keep me
as before, then
bless me in eternity,
comfort and remember me.

Welcome me now
my soul returns,
oh, blessed place
for which it yearns,
lasting peace and glory be,
welcome, welcome me.

Reverie

There will come a day, I suppose,
when that photo of us in the kitchen
will not inspire longing. It was Christmas,
many years ago, although I often squander
my moments living there again and again.

We stood with your arm around me
in front of the empty cupboard that
awaited the evergreen boughs
and pine cones and the little toy truck
we picked up at the Silver Moon.

My eye always goes to the way
your hand is clasped so firmly
around my arm. I was yours, after all.
I can still feel the heat and strength
of your fingers, joy on both our faces,
even with all that had gone before,

all that was to come, none of it
of consequence in that single moment
when, click, we were nothing less than
the truest and most joyous of ourselves.

———————•————

Promise

As long as there is daylight,
I will trace the edges of the
clouds with gentle imagining—
angels in flight, the rabbit
and the teddy bear, the puppy
and the face of Moses.

As long as there is a night sky,
I will roam the moonlit heavens
for the comet and the shooting star.

As long as there is rain, I will
relish the trickle and the pour, the
dowsing and the sop that satisfy
Nature's thirst and a heart every-so-
slightly parched by loss and longing.

———◆———

Contrition

If I come to say I'm sorry,
may I come?
May I hold your beauty
in my grateful gaze
and plead acceptance?

If I ask that you forgive me,
may I stay?
May your countenance
fulfill my prayer
and draw me near?

If I dare to say I love you,
may I hope?
May the flame unquenched
by stubbornness and pride
begin to blaze anew?

May I dream?
May I nestle in your
peacefulness, unworthy,
and abide forever
in your merciful love?

May I come?

———◆——

I Would Have Liked It

I would have liked to
share the days with you,
a lifetime of days and
moments; I would have
liked to forever see your
face across the table, your
eyes shining with love
and promise, hands
reaching to me in grace,
but all the chairs are
empty now, save one,
and the eyes I see
across from me are those
in the mirror, and they
promise only reverie which,
at last, is finally enough.

————•————

Oil

Everything squeaks now
and I don't know where to put the oil.
How important a thing
could that have been compared to
choosing just the proper shade of pink
to match a sofa cushion to a curtain flounce?
Or knowing how to apply eyeliner –
no easy thing to lay it thin
against the lashes - and blush
(we used to call it rouge) blending
always blending, so as not to make
a brilliant cheek apple only a clown
could envy. But not a single thought
as to where the oil would one day
have to go to keep a wheel or a hinge
or a bearing from sounding like a small
animal with its foot caught between

rows of iron teeth.

I know other things,
and these, too, are useful, are they not?
Precisely which size container
will hold a quarter pot of lentils or
a half-full skillet of sausage bits?
I can wrap a package, measuring and folding
and cutting with a surgeon's finesse,
nothing wasted or torn. But now I hold
an oil can and listen to my garage door
screaming as it goes, with not one clue
as to where to point the squirt. I expected
there to be a hole for it, but no, there is only
a place for it, mostly undetectable to an eye
trained in ruffled shams and hair gel.
And so I find myself at a loss for keeping
things that are dry or old or merely worn
from grating one upon the other, which
seems to bring us, as everything always
does, back to lost love.

As If One (Nonet)

"I'm afraid he has suffered a stroke."

The words were shrapnel – I was stunned.

"Will he be all right," I asked.

"We'll see," he said. "We'll see."

"What will happen now?"

I asked, as much

About him

As me.

God!

Be a Dear

Let's go into the breakfast room;
It's not so noisy there. No, you're not
keeping me from anything – it's been
like this for weeks, hammering, plastering,
painting. A complete madhouse.
I'm glad you stopped by.

Can I get you some ice tea?
How are Regina and the children? Oh,
that's good to hear – such a lovely family,
David. Your father was so proud. I've
missed you all, but you can see why
I haven't been very social lately.

Yes. And I'm very grateful for the
invitations, believe me. But all of this
has been exhausting and, you're right,
it is quite a change, isn't it? Martin and I
were together three years and he liked
everything just the way it was.

Come in. Would you excuse me
for a minute, David? They never get
things right. We've been going round
and round with the crown molding.
Things that should be so simple,
well, they just never are, are they?

Did we get it right this time, Harlan?
Dear, no, the six-inch molding, not the four.
Yes, please do—we really are wasting
a lot of time on this. I'd like to get it done.
Thank you. And please tell the men to be
careful with their equipment on the new tile.

So, tell me what's been going on, David.
How is everyone? Things are good at
home, I hope. And by the way, that
sweater is the perfect blue for your eyes,
just like your dad, although you do look a bit
tired. You're not working too hard, are you?

But, David, oh my goodness, I don't
understand. The plant closed before
your father died, and that was nearly
eight months ago. You're still looking?
I was sure by now there would be something.
After all, you were a manager.

How I wish I could, David. I really do.
But you can see what I'm dealing with,
and there's just no let up. It's all been
tumbling around me and every bit of it
with a price tag. Just one thing
after another. Absolute mayhem.

Still, let me see what I can do.
Be a dear and hand me my purse.
Your father taught me always to have
one large bill on hand just in case.
I guess this would qualify for what he meant.
And I give it to you with pleasure.

I do wish it could be more, but as I've
said, there's so much on my shoulders
right now, David. And next week it'll be
drapes and plantation blinds. New chairs.
He was a fine man, your father, but never
liked to change a thing, not a thing.

Look at this place, David. Look at what
I'm dealing with. We've every one of us
had our hard times. But it makes us strong,
builds character. Martin didn't make his
fortune young. It is quite possible you will
share that destiny. Be proud and patient.

Tell you what. The new kitchen should be
finished in a few weeks. Why don't you all
plan on coming over for dinner next
month. Tell Regina to not even think about
bringing a thing, just those lovely children.
I have a few recipes I'm dying to try out.

You know how much you mean to me.
I may have come late to the family, but
we're all family nonetheless. Which reminds
me. Your dad's old chair is in the garage,
any time you want to take it. The men can
help you load it now, if that works for you.

Bye, bye, David. Big hug. You are such
a fine man. Martin loved you so. Think
about something part time. You know I'll
help in any way I can. Maybe Regina
can get her library job back. It will all
work out, David. Just you wait.

———•———

October

Homeward now,
the wind against
us brisk, tree tops
flailing untamed
with the darkening
late day gusts;
burnished gold,
smoke-rise and
leaf fall, Chamomile,
and comforter, hot
soup, fireside and
nap time, the summer
spirit, all trumpets,
drum beat and blistered
toes, quieting to a
cadence that suggests
reflection by which
to feed the hungry soul
and restore the dream
of higher self.

Soon it Passes

Soon it passes, the pain subsides,
the longing now and then recedes,
the movie starts, the yard man mows,
the phone rings; there's something
someone needs, and I'm okay, it's okay
really, this is how it comes and goes,
torn and bereft, then a sense that there's
still something left; pain will pass and
no one knows, no one really. No one—or nearly.

———◄•►———

Of Two Minds

There, I've left it all on a cool-silk day,
the fabric of yet another dream,
lavishly supple, smooth.
Then what part makes it bold?
Where is the heat?
Oh, yes, some lamb's wool.
No, the heat of passion.
Okay, red silk. Trashy.
Red wool? Tacky.
Then it must be in the fineness
and the folding.
You know that's not me.
Deep red suede like a saddle blanket?
I'm retiring, not defeating the Huns.
Red velvet, then, like the cake. That's final.
Not crazy about the word final,
but I can live with the cake idea.
And how will you account for new thinking?
That has to be white – clean slate kind of stuff.
Maybe charcoal gray for chalkboard?

I'm back in school? Wake up,
I'm throwing off all rules, remember?
Okay, it's got to be blue for sky's the limit.
Limit is a rule.
Oh, just blue then.
Deep, bright, baby, powder, electric.
All the blues there are.
The blues? Seriously? You going down that road?
Well, there might be some of that.
Then how about black. Just go ahead, black!
No, maybe just some dark blue, that's all.
You can live with a little dark blue,
midnight blue even, just hours before
the sky lightly pinkens for the new day.
Or would that be yellow?
No rules, remember?
But that pink part is sailor-take-warning.
Then how nice that I'm not planning to be a sailor.

Up

Spouses once knew how
to put up with each other;
they rarely just gave up.

We liked it when people stood up
for what they believed; we
admired a stand-up kind of guy.

No matter what, we shaped up
and respected someone
we could look up to.

Some went up the ladder,
some went up the river
some were just not up to it,
but in time proved to be
upstanding all the same.

The up-starts could be trouble,

always up to something;
they soon would have to face up
to life's real challenges—put up
or shut up. It's always up to us.

————•————

Say Something

I was, like,
I can't even,
ya know, I mean,
like, so there he is
and I, like, look
and he's, ya know,
like right there,
I mean like, seriously?
and he, like, walks over,
I mean, like ya know.
And I can't even,
I'm like, like
speechless.

Wholesome Fears

I miss those old-time childhood
fears, back in the day when women
had names like Miriam, Edith, Edna
and Bess. Something scary was
under every kid's bed or in their closet.
Mine was that big guy with the block
shoes and the bolt in his neck who
stood in a dark corner, though no one
ever believed me. It never helped that he
disappeared when my mother turned on
the light. But it didn't matter, I guess,
because as soon as she did, I fell asleep.

Those childhood monsters were kind of
wholesome, in a way. I saw Boris Karloff
on TV one time and he seemed like a
pleasant enough guy in real life. When I
was bad, my father threatened me with a
thwack across the rear end with his belt;

some threat but back then, it worked,
especially when he followed through.

That and diagramming a sentence in front of
the whole class were the scariest things I
knew of in that safe little world before
transfats and terrorism. There's nothing
scary under my bed anymore, unless
you count the treasures my cat might
drag in and deposit there; still, it's
sometimes harder to fall asleep when
I consider that our grown-up monsters
don't scare off so easy, even with the light on.

————•,————

A Valentine Sonnet, Seriously?

Let me be the knight your heart has craved.
I do not have a fine white horse on which to ride,
I have no list of damsels I have saved,
I have no sword and scabbard at my side.

But I can slay the dragon of your fears,
And I can keep the darkest clouds at bay.
I'll kiss away your every frown, your tears,
I'll bring the joy, the sunlight to your day.

I'll find the strength I need within your eyes,
My fortitude will come from your sweet touch,
Your kiss will always make me realize
No other love could mean so very much.

So, promise me the charms my heart adores,
And once you sign the pre-nup, I am yours.

————◆———

The Fall of the Year

I make my way to where
the bronze woods blaze,
to the wending roads in
solace, and meet myself
in the dancing flames,
there to remember the fire.
Like voices of the seraphim,
the melody sings my
youth, for soon the dry
curled leaves will fall to the
wind's compelling whistle.

Irma

The ripping swirls of wind
The howling drench of gales
The savage roar of tides

The power failed at once
The darkness fraught with fear
By Grace, the house survived

———•———

Safe Deposit

I opened the old cigar box
the other day, its sweet aroma
of cotton lint so familiar to your
beauty, and found the spools
of thread you used to mend
Daddy's navy trousers, my
school uniform, your apron.

Among the half-filled bobbins,
a faded piece of yellowed paper
bore the Butterick pattern number
of my prom dress, and pinned to it
a snippet of pink organza.

One thin skein of hunter green
remained from the needlepoint
that hangs above my desk.

I put your silver thimble on my finger
to once again feel your sweetness.

Lovelorn

Dear Heartbroken,
allow me to respond from personal experience.
No. Why get into all that.
Don't even go there.

Dear Heartbroken,
forgiveness is a rich and soulful virtue.
When we forgive, we heal and grow, we...
Blah, blah, blah, blah, blah, blah, blah.

Dear Heartbroken,
a wise person once said...
Hmmm, where is that stupid quote
about betrayal.

Dear Heartbroken,

you were smart to talk it over with him.

Any man can stumble once in a while.

You showed maturity in keeping an open mind.

Really? I mean really?

Dear Heartbroken,

ditch the louse.

———•,——

Mortal Time

I came and in my coming I became
this siphoned bit, this particle, by
earthly name described, and for mere
consequence, merely and no more,
then parting as one parts through
Heaven's door, all the time,
and yet no time at all, a rising flame,
flickering, flickered, small, burning
still as only ash and ember burn,
learning less and ever less as ever
learners learn—starting out and
ending up entirely the same.

———◄•►———

Leaf

Faded gold and silent
as a last breath,
the sacramental hush
of final parting,
the downward drift,
the easy sway
of a sacred dance,
too full of Nature's
divine purpose
to be so casually
regarded as while
drying a dish
or hanging a sock,
but to be held instead
by an artist's deft stroke
or a poet's lyric word
on parchment,
everlasting.

Labor Day

They fixed each other's wagons,
and built each other's barns;
they bought land with a prize
bull and made supper from the
dove they killed with the shotgun
they got when they turned nine,
they traded milk for corn and eggs
for flour and kicked the can down
the road because it was their only
toy and never had trouble getting
their arms around anything, even a
feisty steer or a screw-wormed calf.

They spoke little but said a lot,
and the only thing they ever walked
back was a stray heifer. They didn't
get their motivation from a seminar,
website, CD, workshop, you-tube,
tape or tweet, from a preacher,
maybe, from some homegrown

sensibility, likely. They suffered
a will and an intellect born of the
vagaries of man and nature. They
would all have been on the same
page if they'd had the time to read
or knew how. At the end of the day
they went to bed.

———••———

Cold Autumn

Ah, the lengthening dark,
when the canopies whirl
in the long slant of shadows,
and the wind—oh, that wind—
with its bellowing wheeze
that rivals the teakettle's whistle.

My nostrils flare from
the sweet tang of leaf-burn;
the snap of the hearth
fills my ready ear with song,
and the warm flannel coverlet
calls me to slumber;

I will doze in the armchair
a book in my lap; while
my sleepy-eyed cat
purrs in peace by the fire.
We will cozy together
awaiting the frost.

« The Avocet Poetry Journal

Turnips

I thought of you today
when I fixed the turnips
that made the house
smell of Thanksgiving;
you, there in your apron,
glasses steamed from
the open oven door, dots
of gravy on the stove top,
a pie, a pot, a dish, a cake,
candied yams and onion peel—
sweetness and tears.

Here for a time

One day soon the sun will set
on yet another person's folly,
yet another person's toil;
isn't it always ours to choose
how we come by what we gain,
how we deal with what we lose?

How much did he leave?
They asked when he was gone
He left it all, they said,
he left it all

———•———

Just That Quick

Ten minutes before he died,
he took another sip of coffee
then placed the thermal mug
back in the cup holder; traffic
was moving well—he'd be
grateful to finish the installation
early and get to his son's
soccer game on time for once;

Five minutes before he died
he thought again about what
to get his wife for her birthday;
he never was much good at
buying gifts and stuff—she was
the one who always did that; he'd
have to stop by the mall tomorrow
after his doctor's appointment.

Two minutes before he died
traffic was picking up,

everybody in a hurry, but he'd
stay where he was, keeping the
old flatbed right there in the
middle lane, no need to rush;
let the idiots fight it out trying
to get ahead of the pack.

One minute before he died
his cell phone rang; whoever
it was would have to leave a
message; he never did like
talking on his cell phone while
driving, you get too involved;
and now the texts started—
maybe a change in plans.

Ten seconds before he died,
he looked down.

Anzio

Ahh, so very long ago,
and yet I can still see it—
that little table in the breezeway,
our favorite. Remember?
How silly to think you could.

Ancient Botticino stone at our feet,
and overhead a fuchsia bough—
the scent of sweet wisteria
that would have to last a lifetime.
Mine, not yours.

Beyond us, the glistening waters
of the Tyrrhenian Sea,
as yet undefiled, waiting.
How apropos, the weeping fig.

«Quill and Parchment

For Calm

Help me to listen for you, Oh Lord;
I lose your voice in the groans
of my own longing, I miss your word
in the frantic wishfulness of my heart;
open my ears, Dear Jesus, and
whisper me your name; let it thunder
gently in the silence of my soul,
like the rush of distant water,
let it sing to me, let it beckon me,
and let me come.

———•———

Spectre

My friend died today.
I liked her so much,
loved her really.
Such a loss.

It's hard to fathom
those empty spaces
left by friends
now gone.

Like musical chairs,
one then another
removed until
there are two of us
and only one last breath.

Water

They seep into our thoughts, those dreams,
like the steady trickle of a leaky hose or the
menacing torrent from the breach of a dam,
one way or another, unable to be held back
by reasoning, rectitude, noble sacrifice or
downsized hopes. By giving up or letting go.

An unfamiliar species springs up in the garden
and you wonder is it a weed, too beautiful to
just kill off outright? Would watering it be a
terrible waste? Would potting it be absurd?
If someone saw, would you have to explain
yourself or just turn off the spigot? Yank it
out by the roots or it comes back like a
cancer cell or the recollection of a child's
laughter, consuming. It seeks all, like life
itself, soaked to the core with longing.

———◄•►———

1405 Wheeler Road

If you listen
with a proper heart,
you can hear it ticking
from the Interstate,
alive with time
and its painful flow,
things that came
that needed to go
a little too soon
or much too late,
a place past waiting
lost in the wait.

For Irmgard

Lovely Flower,
you have bloomed
in a radiant light,
your beauty has made
an enchanted garden.

Loveliest of flowers,
your fragrance
will linger
forever.

The Hour Glass

When I saw you
white, life going,
felt the cold, smooth
hand unfeeling,
stroked the silver
of your unreddened brow,
I knew – this was the first
of the last of you,
and with your passing
my passing too;
at least the me
there was till now.
I couldn't help
but wonder how
the world itself
was still intact,
earth still turning
now that it lacked
your fire,
and everything

that went before –
Pharaohs, Zsu-Zsu
crackers, war,
subways, smiles
and reprimand poured
through this moment
before they fanned
into eternity;
the same and yet
not quite the same
in coming as in going,
as similar before and since
as once had known
and knowing.

———•———

One

You come to that time
when you tend your own
cuts and try to lift both
ends of the rod to hang
the curtain. On waking,
you're sure you've heard
the cupboard door
bumping shut as it once
had; the phantom aroma
of coffee, the hospitable
clink of cup and spoon.

At times like this—
no there is only one time
like this, and it is likely
the remainder of your days—
you're grateful for the ease
you feel being alone but not
lonely, now that the alluring
fragrance of wishfulness has

faded and only the comforting
scent of recollection remains.
Peace can be a most acceptable
substitute for happiness.

October Wind - *Haiku*

Listen at twilight
The trees will sing—
Autumn sonata

Window Table

A weeping ilex scratches on the pane
while the heavens turn to iron;
no spikes of sunlight warm my cup
no robins fill my ear with song,
but the crystal forest quiets the soul,
and a berry flames the garden where
the myrtle has gone to wood;
there is no place for discontent
in a heart so full of wintry wonder.

« The Avocet Poetry Journal

Coming In

We pushed through in a frigid swirl,
stamping our boots on the runner in
the hall, winter hanging on us like a
playful child who would not listen or let go.

We peeled away our dampened caps,
as melting slivers dribbled to the floor
from the straggly fringes of our hair.
Too soon, we tried the buttons
of our coats, our fingers stiff with cold,
our ears red-rimmed with icy burn.

Toby sat up smartly at a distance,
eyeing us with feline prudence,
then licked a paw and sidled off,
while Max wagged and sniffed around us,
tugging at the stray end of a scarf.

We gasped and sighed and laughed,
pecking at the fingers of our gloves,

our words squeezed sideways
through near-frozen lips.
We could hardly feel our noses, yet
we knew the welcome aroma of soup
and warm buttered rolls and home.

« The Avocet Poetry Journal

Wintry

A flap of wings,
the screech
of a hawk echo
through the
sacred silence
of the still and
leafless wood,
then nothing.

As with divine
knowing, Nature
waits in fallow glory.

———•———

Germaine's

Long before the winding paths of
Prospect Park had come to know the
speed and tumble of a skate board or
a roller blade, there was Germaine's—
big and full of stuff and color, bigger
than the Five and Ten and the entire
first floor of the Williamsburg bank.

Wide double doors swept open to my
child's mind—shine and shimmer and
things to touch, candy, nuts and toys;
a glass counter filled with trays of
marshmallow squares and jelly bars
and the scent of toasted coconut.

My mother searched the bolts of fabric
in the shop next door, while I ran my
fingers over aisles of fur and felt and
red things with glitter, twinkle lights
all sparkle and glow, Santa hats and

fake poinsettias, bubble glass
candles and tinsel, and wreaths
that looked like evergreen.

On the mezzanine just past the
furniture displays, Santa on his gilded
throne smiled and nodded at my wish,
then sent me off with a hearty laugh
and a candy cane, Gene Autry's
reindeer lyrics ringing through the store.

This could be the year I got the BB gun
— I always thought so, but the green
cardboard suitcase would do as well or
the thirty-piece plastic farm town that
came with a white rail fence and a church
with cellophane stained-glass windows.

Before we knew it, those shelves would
be stacked with straw hats and sandals
and dreams of the Brighten Beach to
Coney Island with their lure of The Ferris
Wheel and Cyclone, Nathan's and the
midway and Fourth of July fireworks over
the ocean, enough to hold me until the
magic of December came back round again.

———•,———

The Greatest of Early Disappointments

It was not that the boy didn't like me,
none of the boys I liked liked me back.
I didn't know the ways of things, how
to toss a curl or dip a shoulder. No
flirty smile like other girls, who really
didn't like me either. My dresses were
clean and starched and sometimes
the same dresses and maybe more than
once in the same week. But it wasn't that.

And it wasn't because I didn't get the pony
or the bb gun. Okay, well, maybe the bb gun,
just a little. I'd had my hopes, but living one
flight up on a busy avenue, did I really think
I was going to get a horse or a gun? I wasn't
even allowed to have a bike or a dog for fear
that they would find their way into the path
of the uptown bus and me along with them—
my parents' fear, not mine. No, it wasn't that.

It was about the gray stone house with the
slate roof and the wooden shutters, white
trimmed windows and a curvy-topped
front door that made it look like a storybook
cottage. The light from inside was soft amber
behind white crisscross sheers that fluttered
with the breaths I took watching from the
bus stop each morning before school. I could
see that there were bookshelves inside and
rounded cozy-looking chairs like where Mama
Bear and Papa Bear would sit—a living photo
presupposing attributes assigned by my
imagination.

Peggy Larsen lived there, a cheerleader
in my gym class who somehow became a
friend but not because of what my aunt said
about Peggy knowing she looked even better
when she was with me. Peggy invited me over
and I made my way up the flagstone walk
like Dorothy on her way to Oz, like a

princess headed through a storybook door.

I supposed it could have been what I had
imagined. It could have been, but it wasn't.
They had a cat or maybe more than one,
maybe even an unwashed dog somewhere,
although not having a dog I didn't know
what that would smell like. My heart sank.

The seats of those cozy looking chairs were
ever-so-slightly ragged from clawing.
The rug looked clean but worn and each of
the burners on the kitchen stove had a ring of
grime. True, not a very thick ring, so they must
have tried because there was a violin on the
dining room table, after all. Still, the sink
was half-full of dishes and the wallpaper faded.

Two of the chairs held disheveled piles of
books, some of them having spilled onto
the floor near the kitty litter box. Brilliant
people lived here. Brilliant and accomplished
people who could afford to live in such a
neighborhood, and own a violin, a place
to make a child wonder in envy from the
bus stop what it might be like to have an
upstairs bedroom. People like Peggy herself
who had made the cover of *Seventeen*
Magazine as the Clearasil Girl of the Month.
Even so, I felt as low as their enchanting pitched
roof. No, the greatest of early disappointments
had nothing at all to do with a pony.

------◆------

Levittown Christmases

I liked it at Christmas when
everyone slept over. I would
open my eyes to the scent of
bacon and the sight of Lollipop
wagging his tail too close to the
tinsel. Someone had already been
out and back with jelly doughnuts,
crumb buns and crullers,
the funny sheets had been read
and a ham was in the oven.
I wonder still where everyone slept,
how they got up so early and who
woke them? I had been allowed
to stay up late but fell asleep
to their card-playing antics,
laughter and talk of things
I didn't understand and of people
I didn't know. Where did
they sleep, all eleven of them,

in that two-bedroom house,
whose size would not double
for ten more years and half again
years later, whose attic you could
only, as yet, fall through? When
had my mother changed my clothes
and tucked me in, wrapping me in
that cozy flowered quilt on the heated
floor? Things were simpler in those
days, people say.
We had traveled from Brooklyn,
two subway trains and the railroad,
changing at Jamaica station,
three-plus hours, freezing cold,
one small cardboard suitcase,
a Macy's shopping bag filled with
brightly wrapped packages, and a
white cake box double-tied with string.
Year upon year, no one ever did not come.
What did they know that we don't?

We who choke now on the season with
our frantic lives and dreaded plans,
two cars, four bedrooms and three
baths but no room, no time and no will.
It strikes me as such a puzzling thing to
not want to put out even some small
effort for a bit of chaotic enchantment.

———————•,———————

When They Were All Still Here

When they were all still here,
there were many—aunts, uncles,
cousins—time after time, at Christmas,
for example, with its goodwill, gifts and
whispers in the kitchen, fables and faces
immune to the passing of the years.

A knock on the door, then the scramble
of excited voices coming in on a sudden
rush of winter cold, brown paper shopping
bags weighed down with presents and a
white cake box double tied with string.

Tinsel, wreaths, pine cone garlands, ribboned
candy in a crystal dish, a Douglas fir in a
corner of the room, bubble candle lights and
painted glass balls, evergreen, food and family
history, some of which might have been true.

When they were all still here, they spoke of

things and times past, laughing at their own
foolishness or pain, oftentimes with some
odd reasoning, their tales like half-told
secrets beyond my young mind, but I smiled
just the same at the mystery of it all and the fun,
now and then even with a sense of...I don't know...
awe perhaps, at lives stitched ever so tightly
together with affection and selective recall.

Now in my own late years, I've come to know
them better than when they were all still here.

———◄•►———

Legacy

There is such sad beauty in the world
such melancholy riches—
not even so much as a child's tear
or a soldier's casket
but some grip of leaden spirit
that causes the heart to clutch
at the sight of a single leaf
drifting to the ground in autumn
or a note scribbled behind
the wallpaper, an old hammer with
a wooden handle worn in the shape
of a grip—and whose grip could
that have been and what did they
build or patch that may still be here
long after they themselves are gone?
Who was it put those screws in the
old trunk or fixed the latch? There is
a certain touching allure in the very

notion that the recollection of an
entire life might be held in the
threads of a cherished needlepoint
or a fable scrolled on a crusty page.

———◄•►———

For Acceptance

I come to you, Lord,

and the spirit in me is heavy;

I am sad for the dream

that faith has not fulfilled,

for the one that faith

has not compelled,

for the love that faith

has not returned,

for the heart that faith

has not repaired,

for the grief that faith

has not assuaged,

for the loss that faith

cannot undo;

and yet...

and yet...

Faith – nonetheless and true.

———◂•▸———

Winter Morning - Haiku

White-whiskered grass
Gun-metal heavens
Blissful and bleak

Making Up the Bed

Snowing harder now,
the roads are bad—
family staying over;

Ahh, new sheets.
How long have we had these?
Soft creases hurled against
the air that quickly smells
of cotton and sweet soap;
sheen and supple weave.

Delightful chaos—
leftovers, levity
and high thread count.

———•———

Christmas Boxes

How well I recall the old boxes
where we kept the things for the tree;
a grocery carton marked Alphabet Soup
was where the lights would be.
The balls that we wrapped in tissue
were packed in a wooden case
that bore the faded stenciled words,
Antique Bobbin Lace.

A worn and tattered shoebox
was where we kept the star,
the angel was stored in a box that read,
The World's Renowned Cigar.
Each of the fragile ornaments
was laid in a painted chest—
it belonged to my Grandpa's mother,
that's why I liked it best.

Our precious Christmas treasures
we stored from year to year
in those old familiar boxes
that we came to hold so dear;
So, pass me the tape for patching—
there's a lid that's coming apart,
and I'll keep that box a dozen more years,
and a hundred more in my heart.

Goals

Think of walking twenty miles
And ten won't seem so many;
Think of walking thirty-five
And you won't walk any.

Counsel

If you want to learn it, teach it,
If you want to pass it, reach it,
If you want to get it, give it,
If you want to be it, live it.

A Toast

I wish you joy and beauty,
I wish you time and hope,
and all good thoughts
and all good things
for you to have and give;
I wish you calm and vigor,
I wish you wise and well;
a merry heart, a merry home
and faith-filled years to live.

———•———

Orare

Lord, I pray, instill in me
a sense of purpose, curiosity—
to learn, to think, to try, to do—
then, Lord, may I ask of you
a sense of hope that I may never lose
and time, Lord, not to spend, but use.

———•———

About the Author

Mary Flynn is an award-winning author of poetry and fiction. Her writing is an imaginative mix of humor, pathos and irony that explore the human experience, often with a surprising twist.

As a full-time staff writer for Hallmark Cards in Kansas City, Mary wrote for every category of Hallmark greetings as well as Hallmark's special poetry collections.

Since then, Mary's observational humor has appeared in the *Sunday New York Times, Newsday* and other dailies and magazines. She was a poetry prizewinner in the *Writer's Digest* Writing Competition, a double finalist in the Royal Palm Literary Awards, and her short story, "Jeremiah's Orchard," is published in *The Saturday Evening Post Anthology of Great American Fiction.*

Mary recently retired from her international speaking role with Disney to write full-time. "Confessions of a Hallmark Greeting Card Writer" is Mary's fun opportunity to present an engaging program that delights her audiences with the how-to as well as the mishaps behind the scene.

Her debut novel, *Margaret Ferry*, which has a five-star rating on Amazon, won the Gold Medal in fiction, the Silver Medal in Religious writing and the Silver Medal in Christian writing. Her most recent release, also an award-winner, is *Disney's Secret Sauce—the-little-known factor behind the business world's most legendary leadership*, already enjoying five stars on Amazon.

To find out more about
Mary's books and talks please visit »

———————•—————

www.MaryFlynnWrites.com

———————•—————

76957164R00096

Made in the
USA
Columbia, SC